Colorado
The Centennial State

Jason Glaser

PowerKiDS
press™

New York

To my brother, Scott, and to the Colorado Rapids soccer team, who always put on a good show

Published in 2010 by The Rosen Publishing Group, Inc.
29 East 21st Street, New York, NY 10010

First Edition

Editor: Amelie von Zumbusch
Book Design: Greg Tucker
Photo Researcher: Jessica Gerweck

Photo Credits: Cover © Grafton Smith/Corbis; p. 5 Bob Thomason/Getty Images; p. 7 James Thomas Thurlow/George Eastman House/Getty Images; pp. 9, 15 Tyler Stableford/Getty Images; pp. 11, 13, 17, 22 (tree), 22 (animal), 22 (flag), 22 (flower) Shutterstock.com; p. 19 © Atlantide Phototravel/Corbis; p. 22 (bird) © www.iStockphoto.com/Cindy Creighton; p. 22 (Ruth Handler) Ron Galella/WireImage/Getty Images; p. 22 (Byron White) David Hume Kennerly/Getty Images; p. 22 (Chauncey Billups) Andrew D. Bernstein/NBAE/Getty Images.

Library of Congress Cataloging-in-Publication Data

Glaser, Jason.
  Colorado : the Centennial State / Jason Glaser. — 1st ed.
      p. cm. — (Our amazing states)
  Includes index.
  ISBN 978-1-4358-9344-3 (library binding) — ISBN 978-1-4358-9776-2 (pbk.) —
ISBN 978-1-4358-9777-9 (6-pack)
  1. Colorado—Juvenile literature. I. Title.
  F776.3.G536 2010
  978.8—dc22
                                        2009024999

Manufactured in the United States of America

CPSIA Compliance Information: Batch #WW10PK: For Further Information contact Rosen Publishing, New York, New York at 1-800-237-9932

Contents

On Top of America   4
One Hundred Years of Freedom   6
The Rocky Mountains   8
The Ups and Downs of Colorado   10
Other Life in Colorado   12
Making Money   14
The Mile-High City   16
History in the Parks   18
Fun for All Seasons   20
Glossary   21
Colorado at a Glance   22
Index   24
Web Sites   24

On Top of America

Colorado is one of the highest American states. No part of the state is lower than 3,280 feet (1,000 m) above sea level. While the whole state is high, Colorado's highest points are its mountains. People in Colorado talk about the fourteeners, or mountains that are taller than 14,000 feet (4,267 m). That is more than 2.5 miles (4 km) up! Colorado is home to more than 50 fourteeners.

An imaginary line called the Continental **Divide** runs through Colorado's Rocky Mountains. It divides the United States into two parts. All the rain and snow that falls west of this line ends up in the Pacific Ocean. Rain and snow that falls to the east ends up in the Atlantic Ocean or the Gulf of Mexico.

This hiker is enjoying a view of Pike National Forest. The forest is home to several of Colorado's fourteeners, including its most famous mountain, Pikes Peak.

One Hundred Years of Freedom

In 1776, the United States broke away from England and became a free country. At that time, a people called the Utes lived in the eastern Rocky Mountains. France and Spain both claimed land on which the Utes lived. However, the Utes often fought with other Native Americans and were hard to control. Both countries decided to sell that troubled land to the United States.

American settlers soon arrived on the Utes' land. The settlers called the land the Colorado **Territory**. When enough people lived there, the settlers voted to become a state. Colorado became a state on August 1, 1876. Since Colorado became a state 100 years after the United States formed, it is called the **Centennial** State.

Chief Ouray of the Utes (center) was known as a peaceful leader. He visited Washington, D.C., in the 1860s to try to keep Ute land safe from American settlement.

The Rocky Mountains

Colorado's Rocky Mountains are part of a long mountain chain. The Rockies formed **millions** of years ago, when two of Earth's **continental plates** pushed against each other. One plate was pushed up and broke apart, forming the Rockies.

The Rockies lie in waves across Colorado. Rivers wrap around the mountains. Trains pass through low valleys between mountain **ranges**. Train travelers can see the many pine, aspen, and fir trees that grow on the Rockies. Climbers in the mountains may spot the state flower, columbine, and other wildflowers that grow there. Visitors can also see **fossils** in the rock that makes up the mountains. The fossilized remains of many dinosaurs have been found in Colorado.

Many people visit Colorado every year to go skiing in the Rockies. Some of the most popular ski slopes are in Aspen, where these children are skiing.

9

The Ups and Downs of Colorado

The mountains play an important part in bringing water to Colorado. The high mountaintops get snow all year long. When this snow melts, it runs into rivers that wash down the mountains. Rivers that flow westward pass through high, flat **mesas** and warm valleys. The rivers that flow east pass over land that looks like a long, flat ramp. This land, called the Front Range, lies between the mountains and the eastern plains. Eastern Colorado's plains have dry **prairies** with tall grass.

Weather can change quickly in Colorado. It also changes over short distances. It could be snowing on top of a mountain, raining partway down the mountain, and sunny at the bottom!

This is Monument Canyon, in western Colorado. It was made by the Colorado River, which ate away at rock mesas over thousands of years until deep valleys formed.

Other Life in Colorado

The plants and animals of Colorado are as different from place to place as the land is. On the plains, coyotes, foxes, and jackrabbits run through plants, such as sagebrush and cacti. Big mountain goats live high on the mountains. On the mountainsides, black bears can be found among the aspen and spruce trees. Bobcats and mountain lions live in the mesas and hills. Up above, bald eagles fly over them all.

The state animal of Colorado is the Rocky Mountain bighorn sheep. These animals move easily over the stony mountaintops. In the fall, the mountains ring with the sound of male sheep hitting their horns together. The males do this to get the attention of female sheep.

A male bighorn sheep's horns can weigh up to 30 pounds (14 kg)! The sheep have hard bones in their heads, so they do not get hurt when they ram into each other.

Making Money

In the past, settlers came to Colorado to mine for gold but stayed for the view. Today, people in Colorado make money from both mining and beautiful views. Companies mine coal and strong metals. Visitors spend money to ski, hunt, fish, and climb in Colorado's mountains. In the state's cities, travelers eat fine food and go to fun shows.

Colorado is home to farmers who raise cows and pigs. Other farmers grow crops, such as corn, beans, and potatoes. Businesses build special parts for aircraft, computers, **scientific** tools, and other machines. At the Denver Mint, in Denver, Colorado, people create money by stamping coins. If your coins have a tiny *D* on them, they were made in Denver!

Colorado has been home to cattle ranchers, like this man, for about 150 years. Cattle ranchers raise cows for their meat on big farms called ranches.

The Mile-High City

Denver is the largest city in Colorado. It was the capital of the Colorado Territory and became the capital of the state, too. Denver lies 1 mile (1.6 km) above sea level. This earned Denver the nickname the Mile-High City.

The air in Denver is thinner than the air in lower places is. Air in high places is always a bit thinner. People who are new to Denver must get used to breathing less **oxygen**. Some people believe visiting sports teams have a harder time playing in Denver because of the thin air. The **professional** football, baseball, hockey, and basketball players who work in Denver are already used to the air. Some Denver fans think this gives their teams an edge.

Denver was founded as a small mining settlement during the gold rush of 1858. Today, the city has many tall buildings, parks, theaters, and restaurants.

History in the Parks

Colorado has many interesting national parks. Some teach you about the state's past. Colorado's past goes back to before the Utes. A people known as the Ancestral Pueblos lived there hundreds of years ago. No one knows where they went, but you can learn about them at Mesa Verde National Park. The houses they built in the cliffs are still there today. One spot, Long House, may have been home to 150 people.

One of Colorado's newest national parks, Great Sand Dunes National Park and Preserve, looks like a giant sandbox. However, it is really a desert hidden in the mountains. People who like water might want to visit Rocky Mountain National Park. The huge park holds many beautiful lakes, rivers, and waterfalls.

Around 600 homes have been found built into the cliffs of Mesa Verde National Park. The Ancestral Pueblos lived there between the years 600 and 1300.

Fun for All Seasons

It is easy to see why people love Colorado. Even in the state's busy cities, people can see beautiful mountain **peaks** covered with snow. In the winter, you can visit Colorado's snowy mountains to go skiing, snowboarding, and snowshoeing. You can also travel to places below the peaks that are still warm enough for hiking, rafting, fishing, or horseback riding. If you get tired from all this exercising, Colorado has more than 20 hot springs in which you can **relax**.

At Dinosaur National Monument, near Dinosaur, Colorado, you can see the bones of hundreds of dinosaurs stuck in the rocks. Many visitors to Colorado have decided never to leave. Maybe the dinosaurs felt that way, too!

Glossary

centennial (sen-TEH-nee-ul) Having to do with a hundredth anniversary.

continental plates (kon-tuh-NEN-tul PLAYTS) The moving pieces of Earth's outside.

divide (dih-VYD) Something that breaks something else apart.

fossils (FO-sulz) The hardened remains of dead animals or plants.

mesas (MAY-suhz) Hills or mountains with flat tops.

millions (MIL-yunz) Thousands of thousands.

oxygen (OK-sih-jen) A gas that has no color or taste and is necessary for people and animals to breathe.

peaks (PEEKS) The very tops of things.

prairies (PRER-eez) Large places with flat land and grass but few or no trees.

professional (pruh-FESH-nul) Having to do with people who are paid for what they do.

ranges (RAYN-jez) Rows of mountains.

relax (ree-LAKS) To feel loose and to let go of tightness, nervousness, or worry.

scientific (sy-en-TIH-fik) Having to do with studying the world.

territory (TER-uh-tor-ee) Land that is part of a country but is not a state or province.

Colorado State Symbols

State Tree
Colorado Blue
Spruce

State Animal
Rocky Mountain
Bighorn Sheep

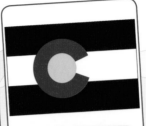
State Flag

State Bird
Lark Bunting

State Flower
White and Lavender
Columbine

State Seal

Famous People from Colorado

Ruth Handler
(1916–2002)
Born in Denver, CO
Inventor of the
Barbie Doll

Byron White
(1917–2002)
Born in Fort Collins, CO
Supreme Court Justice

Chauncey Billups
(1976–)
Born in Denver, CO
Basketball Player

Colorado State Map

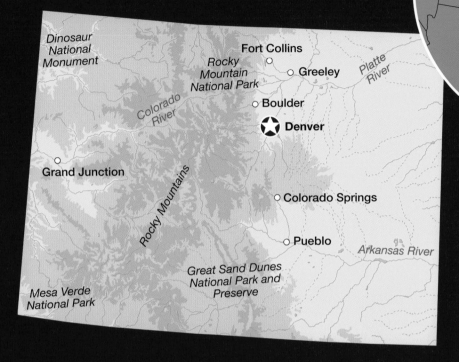

Dinosaur National Monument

Fort Collins

Rocky Mountain National Park

Greeley

Platte River

Colorado River

Boulder

⭐ Denver

Grand Junction

Rocky Mountains

Colorado Springs

Pueblo

Arkansas River

Great Sand Dunes National Park and Preserve

Mesa Verde National Park

Legend

○ Major City

⭐ Capital

〰 River

Colorado State Facts

Population: About 4,301,261

Area: 104,247 square miles (269,999 sq km)

Motto: "Nil Sine Numine" ("Nothing Without the Deity")

Songs: "Where the Columbines Grow," words and music by A. J. Fynn, and "Rocky Mountain High," words by John Denver and music by Mike Taylor

Index

B
businesses, 14

C
Colorado Territory, 6, 16
Continental Divide, 4
continental plates, 8

E
England, 6

F
fossils, 8
fourteeners, 4
France, 6

G
Gulf of Mexico, 4

H
hot springs, 20

L
land, 6, 10

M
mesa(s), 10, 12, 18
mountain chain, 8

N
Native Americans, 6

O
oxygen, 16

P
Pacific Ocean, 4

peaks, 20
prairies, 10

R
rain, 4
range(s), 8, 10
Rocky Mountains, 4, 6, 8

S
sea level, 4, 16
settlers, 6, 14
Spain, 6

U
Utes, 6, 18

W
waves, 8

Web Sites

Due to the changing nature of Internet links, PowerKids Press has developed an online list of Web sites related to the subject of this book. This site is updated regularly. Please use this link to access the list:
www.powerkidslinks.com/oas/co/